THE ROYAL NAVY IN AUSTRALIA
1900 - 2000
by Vic Jeffery and Ross Gillett

Two Colossus class light fleet aircraft carriers were completed as maintenance carriers. A "follow on" from the purpose built repair carrier **Unicorn** commissioned earlier in the war. **Perseus** is shown here alongside the Kirribilli "dolphins", with the official residence of the Governor of New South Wales, visible behind her island superstructure. **Perseus** was withdrawn from service in 1954.

(Fleet Air Arm Museum Archive)

Author's Notes

The authors would like to express their thanks to the many individuals and organisations who provided material for this book. Foremost amongst these would be the photographers of the RAN, especially those from years gone by. The Royal Australian Navy has always covered the arrival of friendly and visiting ships and continues to do so today. For the warships of the Royal Navy and the ships of the Royal Fleet Auxiliary, Australian ports have always been their home away from home.

The majority of British warships in Australia visited Sydney or Fremantle, mainly because of the port facilities on the eastern and western seaboards.

Sydney provided this home to the British men-o-war as early as 1788, with a permanent detachment from 1859. Ever since then naval photographers, both official and from the public, captured the presence of hundreds of these ships in Sydney Harbour, their arrivals and departures. After the final departure of the units of the Auxiliary Squadron in the early years of the 20th century and the last ships of the Australia Station in 1912, the Royal Navy was represented in Australian waters by a regular series of visits.

Being Australia's "Western Gateway", understandably the Port of Fremantle features prominently in many of the photographs from Western Australia. Fremantle was the largest Allied submarine base in the Southern Hemisphere between 1942-1945 during which time submarines of the Royal Navy, the United States and Netherlands Navies made many war patrols and carried out special operations. Units of the British Pacific Fleet passed through Fremantle or anchored in Gage Roads in the outer harbour, berths being at a premium in the latter days of the Second World War.

Postwar, both Sydney and Fremantle were gracious hosts to many Singapore-based Royal Navy warships and Royal Fleet Auxiliaries, which were based at the Singapore naval base until Britain's withdrawal from the Far East. Some of the many Fremantle photographs included in this book are from the large collection of images of visiting shipping of all types held by the Fremantle Port Authority.

Some of the fine images included were shot around Fremantle by veteran shiplover and photographer, Mr Walter Murray, now held by the Western Australian Maritime Museum. A photograph of **HMS Hood** entering Fremantle in 1924 is from one of Western Australia's most renowned photographers in the early 20th century, Mr Izzie Orloff.

The book also features many good quality images taken by the photographers of the Royal Australian Navy based in Fremantle and Sydney, most from the early 1970s until the year 2000, with several wartime photographs from the Royal Australian Air Force.

Several photographs are by courtesy of West Australian Newspapers, a respected company that has one of the finest photographic collections in Western Australia. Shiplover Mr Martin Navarro, from the Fremantle Branch of the World Ship Society has kindly shared some of his fine photographs with the authors and they are also reproduced in this book.

In the east, maritime photographers John Mortimer, Chris Sattler and Ron Hart provided many images for the book.

Extensive use was also made of the huge archive of material held by the Fleet Air Arm Museum at Yeovilton, Somerset, and many of their photographs have been reproduced in this book.

Some photographs, now in both authors' collections, cannot be accurately sourced due to a variety of reasons including, being received from unidentified individuals, having no attached details and the passing of time.

First published in the United Kingdom in 2002 by Maritime Books, Lodge Hill, Liskeard, Cornwall, PL14 4EL

The Royal Navy in Australia 1900 - 2000

The naval history of the continent of Australia is as interwoven with that of the Royal Navy as are the proud traditions and customs of the Royal Australian Navy. It is often stated that "Australia was discovered by sailors, explored by sailors and is protected by sailors". A very true statement and one in which the Royal Navy has been a major contributor.

These close bonds are perpetuated with the names of Royal Navy officers from past generations being etched into the history of the Royal Australian Navy.

The Royal Australian Navy College located at Jervis Bay on the southern New South Wales coast, *HMAS Creswell*, honours Captain William Creswell, RN who is recognised as the "father of the RAN". Australia's largest fleet base *HMAS Stirling*, located on Garden Island in Western Australia honours Captain James Stirling, RN who founded the Swan River Colony in 1829. One of Stirling's Captains, Charles Fremantle, has had his name perpetuated by the naming of the nearby major port of Fremantle in his honour.

Other prominent Royal Navy officers whose names are forged in Australia's history include Captain James Cook, Lieutenant Matthew Flinders, Surgeon George Bass and in Papua New Guinea waters, Captain George Moresby. All have had their named perpetuated by having commissioned RAN ships named in their honour. Other RN officers prominent in Australia's early history were the Governors of the Colony of New South Wales, Australia's first naval defender Captain Arthur Philip, Captain William Bligh (formerly of *HMS Bounty*), and other Captains, William Dampier, John Hunter and George Vancouver.

The "First Fleet" ships *HMS Sirius* and *HMS Supply* of 1788 escorted six transports and three supply ships to convey 1480 persons, consisting of 770 convicts, the remainder being Royal Marines or free settlers.

The development of the New South Wales Colony was somewhat slow and the fledgling colony had to fend for itself with the occasional visit by a Royal Navy warship - Britain being heavily preoccupied with the Napoleonic Wars. From 1821 a-man-of-war from the East Indies Station was maintained in Port Jackson in Sydney, usually a 6th rate of sloop, which made occasional visits across the Tasman Sea to inspect the coasts of New Zealand.

Of course, the ongoing task of surveying and charting the waters around the vast continent of Australia had been an ongoing RN commitment since settlement. In the 1840s *HM Ships Alligator*, *Beagle*, *Britomart*, *Fly* and *Rattlesnake* were engaged in marine surveys. By 1850 the Royal Navy force based in the Colony included *HM Ships Calliope* (sailing frigate), *Electra* and *Falcon* (sailing sloops), *Acheron* (paddle sloop), and *Torch* (paddle gun vessel), with the frigate *Herald* engaged on survey duties.

The year 1859 saw the Australia Station established as an independent command. Initially commanded by a Commodore with the Squadron increasing steadily in numerical strength, remaining a collection of diverse types (from up-to-date ships to elderly paddle vessels). The Australia Station was bounded to the north by the parallel of latitude, 10 degrees south, on the first leg of the meridian of longitude, 170 degrees west, on the west of the meridian of longitude 75 degrees east, whilst the southern limit extended south to the Antarctic circle.

This remained unaltered until 1903, when they were extended to embrace the whole of New Guinea, the Caroline and Marshall Island group, and as far eastwards as the Society islands. In 1911 the limits were again modified to cover only the south east coast of New Guinea with New Zealand and all major groups excluding the Loyalty Islands and the New Hebrides.

A Colonial Conference convened in London in 1887 saw various aspects of defence of the empire discussed. One important result of these discussions was the passing of the Australasian Naval Defence Act , under which the Imperial Squadron in Australia was to be augmented by an Admiralty Squadron of five protected cruisers and two torpedo gunboats. This was largely through the efforts and guidance of then Australian Squadron Senior Officer, Rear Admiral George Tryon, RN.

Flagships of the Australia Station during its existence were the sailing frigate (6th rate) *HMS Iris*, screw corvettes *HMS Pelorus* and *HMS Orpheus*, screw frigate *HMS Curacoa*, screw corvettes *HM Ships Challenger, Clio, Pearl* and *Wolverene*, armoured cruisers *HM Ships Nelson, Orlando, Royal Arthur* and *Euryalus*, 1st class protected cruiser *HMS Powerful*, armoured cruiser *HMS Drake*, and the 2nd class protected cruiser *HMS Cambrian*. During the Australia Station's 54 year existence between 25 March 1859 and 21 October 1913, it was commanded by a total of 11 Commodores, seven Rear Admirals, and four Vice Admirals.

During the Great War, the fledgling Royal Australian Navy, led by the new battlecruiser *HMAS Australia*, was placed under the control of the British Admiralty and served predominantly in the northern hemisphere, apart from its first naval action when the light cruiser *HMAS Sydney* despatched the German surface raider Emden at the Cocos Islands in November, 1914.

Between the wars one of the most memorable visits was that of the battlecruisers *HMS Hood* and *HMS Repulse* in 1924 during the Royal Navy's Flag Special Service Squadron world cruise when they visited Fremantle, Albany, Adelaide, Melbourne, Hobart, Jervis Bay and Sydney before crossing the Tasman Sea to visit New Zealand.

Another auspicious occasion was when the heavy cruiser *HMS Sussex* arrived in Australian waters in 1934 flying the Royal Standard of the Duke of Gloucester to carry out two years exchange duty with the heavy cruiser *HMAS Australia*.

The early years of the Second World War saw a limited Royal Navy presence in Australian waters with the old battleship *HMS Ramillies*, along with a handful of cruisers escorting Anzac troop convoys to the Middle East and Singapore. It was not until later in the war in 1944 when the Royal Navy based submarines at the Port of Fremantle in Western Australia, which was the largest Allied submarine base in the southern hemisphere. United States and Netherlands submarines were also operating from the bustling port. Supported by the submarine depot ships *HMS Adamant* and *Maidstone*, 31 Royal Navy submarines operated from Fremantle, the most notable being *HMS Trenchant* which torpedoed and sank the Japanese heavy cruiser *Ashigara* in the Banka Straits on 8 June 1945 making this the largest enemy warship sunk by a Royal Navy submarine in the Second World War.

Royal Navy surface ships returned to Australian waters in numbers with the formation of the British Pacific Fleet in 1944. Commanded by Admiral Sir Bruce Fraser, the first major operation was "Operation Robson", a carrier strike against oil refineries at Belawan Deli, Sumatra on 20 December 1944. The British Pacific Fleet arrived in Sydney on 10 February 1945 and at its peak strength was to eventually number a total of 336 Royal Navy and Commonwealth vessels.

During late 1944, Sydney became the homebase for three new V class submarines, *Voracious*, *Virtue* and *Vox*. To support the boats, the RAN provided the 1922 vintage light cruiser *Adelaide* as an accommodation ship for the three crews.

Postwar saw regular visits from mainly Singapore-based Royal Navy fleet units ranging from aircraft carriers and cruisers to destroyers, frigates and Royal Fleet Auxiliaries. Sydney and Fremantle were their favourite ports of call.

Between 1949 and 1969 a total of 10 Royal Navy submarines; *Thorough*, *Telemachus*, *Tactician*, *Tabard*, *Tapir*, *Trump*, *Taciturn*, *Aurochs*, *Andrew* and *Anchorite* were based in Sydney as the 4th Submarine Flotilla to assist in providing anti-submarine training for the Royal Australian Navy. Normally there were four boats in the flotilla and this was gradually reduced to three, two and finally one, with *HMS Trump* being the last to depart on 10 January 1969, as the new Australian Submarine Squadron expanded in numbers.

The British Monte Bellos Islands atomic tests off the North Western Australian coast in 1952 saw a flurry of Royal Navy activity with the escort aircraft carrier *HMS Campania* as flagship. The River-class frigate *HMS Plym* served as the platform for one of the atomic devices detonated in "Operation Hurricane".

During much of the 1950s and 1960s, the Australian ports of Sydney, Fremantle and Brisbane also played host the Royal Navy's "big" carriers, with names like *HM Ships Albion*, *Centaur*, *Victorious*, *Hermes*, *Ark Royal* and *Eagle* gracing Australian ports in a display of British naval-air power.

With the British withdrawal from Singapore in 1971, the once regular Royal Navy visits slowly decreased, but in the 1980s and early 1990s visits by the Invincible-class aircraft carriers *HM Ships Invincible*, *Illustrious* and *Ark Royal* and their accompanying task groups, brought back memories of a passed era.

Sadly today, other than the occasional visit by a Royal Navy surface ship or a nuclear-powered submarine - all of the latter which berth at *HMAS Stirling* in Western Australia - Royal Navy visits are a rarity, although the bonds remain strong. This book recalls this now bygone era with many nostalgic and memorable photos from the Royal Navy "down under" during the 20th century, in both times of war and peace.

Vic Jeffery and Ross Gillett
2002

HMS Sparrow, a composite gunboat of the Redbreast class seen lying off Port Melbourne, Victoria in 1901. The 805-ton ***Sparrow***, armed with six 4-inch guns and two 3-pounders served on the Australian Station between 1901 - 04.

(Author's collection)

HMS Mohawk, a 1,950-ton Archer class torpedo cruiser rides at her buoy in Sydney Harbour. Armed with six 6-inch guns, eight 3-pounders and three 14-inch torpedo tubes, **Mohawk** served on the Australian Station between 1897-1900.

(Author's collection)

HMS Lizard, a Bramble class composite gunboat, at her buoy in Sydney Harbour. Barquentine-rigged for sail, two 4-inch guns are mounted on the forecastle. The 4-inch guns have been removed from the side-sponsons amidships. The 715-ton **Lizard** served on the Australian Station between 1888-1904.

(Author's collection)

The wooden gun vessel **Dart** rides at its buoy in Sydney Harbour. Displacing 570 tons, **Dart** served on the Australian Station between 1883-1904. It was armed with one 68-pounder gun and two 24-pounder howitzers.

(Author's collection)

HMS Powerful, flagship of the Australia Station in Sydney Harbour. The impressive 14,200-ton first-class protected cruiser arrived on 16 December, 1905 flying the flag of Vice Admiral Sir Wilmot H. Fawkes. After the formation of the Royal Australian Navy on 10 July, 1911, **Powerful** sailed for England on 19 December that same year.　　　　(*Author's collection*)

HMS Pylades, a 1,420-ton Satellite class composite screw sloop (upgraded to corvette) seen in Australian waters (possibly Cairns) during her time on the Australian Station between 1894-1905. ***Pylades*** was armed with fourteen 5-inch guns.

(*Author's collection*)

The third class cruiser *Wallaroo* in Tasmanian waters, during a visit to the island state in 1906. She was one of five cruisers operated by the Royal Navy in Australian waters, as the Commonwealth Naval Forces (1901-1911) comprised mainly coastal patrol and torpedo boats. *Wallaroo* initially arrived in Sydney with the Auxiliary Squadron on 5 September 1891. In July 1900 she was despatched to China for the Boxer Rebellion. The cruiser departed Sydney for last time on 11 January 1906. Paid off and attached to the Devonport harbour establishment **HMS Indus**, she became a guard ship in November 1914, then in March 1919, was renamed *Wallington*. She was sold in February 1920 and broken up by G. Sharpe.

(Author's Collection)

HMS Challenger, a 2nd class cruiser, steams up the tranquil waters of Milford Sound, in New Zealand waters. Her sister ship *Encounter*, in 1912, was transferred to the new Royal Australian Navy. *Challenger* operated in Australian waters from 1904 to 1912, during which time she served in New Zealand waters until July 1905, conducted a lengthy cruise schedule through the South Pacific Ocean islands and in 1911 sailed across the Pacific to visit Chile. She headed back to Portsmouth in July 1912 and arrived home to pay off into reserve on 10 October. After further service in the Great War with the 9th Cruiser Squadron in African waters, she was declared for disposal in 1918 and sold in May 1920, to be broken up by Wards of Preston

(Author's Collection)

An auspicious occasion in Sydney Harbour, circa 1908 with the 3rd class protected cruiser **Pioneer** (left) and the Flagship of the Australian Station, the 1st class protected cruiser **Powerful** both having "Dressed ship" and firing salutes. **Pioneer** was transferred to the fledgling RAN in 1912, sold as a hulk in 1924 and scuttled off Sydney Heads in 1931.

(*Author's collection*)

The Sydney based 3rd class cruiser *Pioneer* during a visit to Tasmania. The small size of *Pioneer* and her sister ships is evident with the crew ranged on the foredeck. The ship enjoyed a long career, with both the Royal Navy and RAN, from November 1900 and from 1 March 1913 to 7 November 1916 respectively. Based on Zanzibar with other British units, *Pioneer* also participated in the blockade against the German cruiser *Konigsberg* in the Rufiji Delta in early 1915. *Pioneer* was sold in 1924. Her stripped hull was towed from Port Jackson in February 1931 and scuttled off the coast of Sydney.

(Author's Collection)

HMS Psyche, a Pelorus class cruiser at anchor during a visit to Port Melbourne in 1914. Having arrived on the Australian Station in 1903, she was one of the first British warships to be equipped with a stockless anchor, which was supplied after her arrival in Australian waters. Commissioned into the Royal Australian Navy on 1 July 1915 **Psyche** was sold on 21 July 1922 for use as a timber lighter and later sank in Salamander Bay, Port Stephen, New South Wales.

(Author's collection)

A picturesque view of the River Derwent in Hobart, Tasmania. Four units of the Royal Navy's Australian Squadron ride peacefully at anchor, including three 3rd class cruisers and the "flagship", the second class protected cruiser ***Cambrian***.

(*Author's Collection*)

HM Ships Torch, ***Ringdove*** and ***Goldfinch*** share the Sutherland Dock on Cockatoo Island in the upper reaches of Sydney Harbour during 1909. The dock was the primary repair/refit facility for the British ships, remaining in use (with the RAN) until the mid-1990s.

(Author's Collection)

The first class protected cruiser *Powerful* was a popular flagship of the Australia Station, serving between 1905 and 1911. She was well armed, carrying two 9.2 inch guns, supported by sixteen 6 inch guns, sixteen 12 pounders, twelve 3 pounders, two Maxims, plus four 18 inch torpedo tubes (below water). In 1908 the flagship sailed across the Tasman Sea to New Zealand with *Encounter* and *Pioneer* to welcome the American Great White Fleet. The US ships later sailed into Sydney, where *Powerful* acted as the centre for all naval and local Government receptions. The cruiser sailed from Sydney for the last time on 19 December 1911, but after arriving at Devonport was laid up from 1913. Relegated to harbour duties, *Powerful* was not sold until August 1929, before being broken up by Hughes Bolckow at Blyth.

(Author's Collection)

The last flagship of the Australian Station, **Cambrian** was also one of the smallest and least powerful flagships. Built as a member of the eight ship Astraea class of Second class protected cruisers. Completed in 1894, **Cambrian** initially operated in the Mediterranean to 1897, then, as part of the Cruiser Training Squadron to 1900. The ship took up station as flagship off the south-east coast of America between 1901 and 1903, followed by the South Atlantic 1903-04. In 1906 she sailed to Australia, including brief service as the Flagship from 1913. After the renaming of the RAN in 1911 (as distinct from the Commonwealth Naval Forces in 1901), **Cambrian** remained based in Sydney until handing over the "flag" to the new battlecruiser **Australia** on 4 October 1913. **Cambrian** sailed back to England on 13 October 1913 and during the Great War was employed as a stokers training ship at Devonport. In March 1916 she was renamed **Harlech**, then **Vivid** in September 1921. She was eventually sold in February 1923 and broken up by Young of Sunderland. (*Author's Collection*)

A fine starboard quarter view of *Hood*, in Sydney Harbour in April 1924. In the background is the Chatham class light cruiser *Sydney*. *Hood's* visit to Sydney was remarkable in two ways. It reinforced the might of the Royal Navy and its capabilities far from home and it provided a stark contrast to the RAN's former flagship *Australia*, stripped as a result of the Washington Naval Treaty and towed out of Sydney to be scuttled on 12 April 1924 in full view of the pristine *Hood*.

(*Author's Collection*)

The battlecruiser **Hood** arriving in Fremantle, Western Australia on 27 February 1924 to a tumultuous welcome during the Royal Navy's "Flag Waving" Special Service Squadron World Cruise of 1923-24. **Hood** was in company with **Repulse**. Both battlecruisers later visited Albany, Adelaide, Melbourne, Hobart, Jervis Bay and Sydney before proceeding across the Tasman Sea to New Zealand.

(*I. Orloff Collection*)

In company with **Hood**, the battlecruiser **Repulse** entering the Port of Fremantle in Western Australia on 27 February, 1924 as part of the Royal Navy's "flag-waving" Special Service Squadron World Cruise. Who could have ever guessed in that time of peace that both of these splendid ships would be sunk 17 years later. (*I. Orloff Collection*)

The County class heavy cruiser *Sussex* arriving in Fremantle on 4 October 1934 flying the Royal Standard from the mainmast as the Duke of Gloucester was embarked. *Sussex* was arriving for a two years exchange service with the heavy cruiser *HMAS Australia*. The large launch in the foreground, *Pollyana*, later saw wartime service with the RAN Auxiliary Patrol in 1943-44 as a coastal patrol vessel before being transferred to the Australian Army as *AM 186*.

(*Author's Collection*)

The heavy cruiser **Dorsetshire** arrives in Sydney for the Sesqui-Centenary celebrations of 1937. Note the amphibian aircraft carried abaft the third stack. Two Dorsetshire class cruisers were completed, as part of the overall County class. After service abroad in the Atlantic, Africa and China stations, *Dorsetshire* was deployed to the South Atlantic from 1940, then the Eastern Fleet in 1942. On Easter Sunday, 5 April 1942, *Dorsetshire* was sunk by Japanese carrier borne aircraft, west of Ceylon, 227 of her crew were lost with the ship.

(Author's Collection)

A member of the fast convoy US.3 carrying Australian and New Zealand troops to the Middle East and sporting its drab wartime grey paint scheme, **HMT Queen Mary** is pictured anchored in Gage Roads in Fremantle's outer Harbour in 1940. She is seen taking on bunkers from the oiler **HMAS Karumba**. On completion, **Queen Mary** and her consorts sailed under the cover of darkness.

(Courtesy of AFA Museum)

An interesting view of the Royal Navy auxiliary cruiser **Maloja** alongside in Fremantle, Western Australia, sporting a broken mast which had crashed down on the ship's bridge - cause unknown. The hull riveting of the 1923-vintage **Maloja**, which carried eight 6-inch guns and two 3-inch, is clearly visible. The 20,914-ton **Maloja** was converted to a troopship in 1941.
(Author's Collection)

The armed merchant cruiser **Hector** in Port Melbourne, Victoria, in 1940 with the RAN sloop **HMAS Yarra** in the foreground. Armed with six 6-inch guns and two 3-inch guns the 11,198 ton **Hector** was later sunk by Japanese carrier borne aircraft on 5 April 1942 at Colombo and written off as a constructive total loss. It was later salved and scrapped in 1946. **HMAS Yarra** was lost in an action against a Japanese heavy cruiser squadron south of Java (after ordering its convoy to scatter) on 4 March, 1942. (*Author's collection*)

A fine view of the P class destroyer **Penn**, when she served as part of the British Pacific Fleet. The ship was armed with four 4-inch guns, mounted in "A", "B", "X" and "Y" positions. **Penn** was initially completed in February 1942. During her 1944 refit in England, **Penn** lost her four single 4-inch guns which were replaced by two twin 4-inch mountings, mounted in "B" and "X" positions. She remained in Australian waters until the end of 1947, when she was reduced to reserve, then scrapped in 1950. (*John Mortimer*)

A brief respite for the Flagship of the British Pacific Fleet, **King George V** and the chance to grant shore leave to her crew as the battleship carried out a refit in the Captain Cook graving dock at the Garden Island Naval Dockyard, Sydney in June, 1945.

(RAN Historical)

A unit of the Sydney-based British Pacific Fleet, the aircraft carrier *Illustrious* entering the Captain Cook graving dock at Garden Island, Sydney to investigate a centre propeller shaft problem, a legacy of a German air attack during a fast convoy to Malta in 1941. The shaft was removed to keep *Illustrious* operational, reducing her maximum speed to 24 knots.

(RAN Historical)

The battleship *Ramillies* in Sydney Harbour in April, 1940 prior to sailing with Convoy US.2 - escorting troopships carrying Australian and New Zealand personnel to the Middle East.
(*Author's Collection*)

A Vickers designed one-man ***Welman*** submarine submerging in Cockburn Sound, Western Australia during a training exercise in 1944. Steered by a joystick, the ***Welman*** was part of the Marine Section of the top secret Services Reconnaissance Department which operated from Careening Bay, Garden Island in Western Australia. (*Author's Collection*)

"High and dry" a British-designed **Welfreighter** four-man transport submarine is seen on its trailer on the shores of Careening Bay, Garden Island, Western Australia. Today the RAN's Fleet Base West, **HMAS Stirling** occupies these very shores.

(*Author's Collection*)

The Royal Navy submarines ***Turpin*** (outboard) and the rather "hawkish" looking ***Tapir*** alongside at North Wharf in Fremantle in 1944. The minelaying submarine ***Porpoise*** is visible in the background on the left. She was later lost on 16 January 1945.

(Author's Collection)

The submarine depot ship **Adamant** alongside at North Wharf in Fremantle, Western Australia in 1945 with three S-class and three of the larger T-class submarines alongside.

(*Author's Collection*)

Units of the British Pacific Fleet in Sydney in 1945. Visible in the busy harbour is the fleet carrier **Formidable** (centre) moving towards its berth. The battleship **King George V** is visible in the Captain Cook Graving Dock (left), whilst a considerable number of RN and RAN destroyers and minesweepers are alongside at Garden Island Naval Dockyard.

(Author's Collection)

The Port of Fremantle in Western Australia was the largest Allied submarine base in the Southern Hemisphere during World War Two. Between 1942-45 some 125 US Navy, 11 Royal Netherlands Navy and 31 Royal Navy submarines made war patrols from the busy port. This 1945 view shows the S-class *Stubborn* in midstream with the T-class boats *Trenchant* (outboard), *Totem*, *Thorough*, and *Taciturn* alongside the submarine depot ship *Adamant*.

(Courtesy of WA Newspapers)

A unit of the British Pacific Fleet, the fleet carrier **Victorious** alongside Victoria Quay in Fremantle Harbour (in February, 1945) after participating in a series of operations against Japanese targets in South East Asia. **Victorious** was enroute to Sydney before joining Task Force 57 for further operations in the Pacific.
(*Walter Murray*)

The T-class submarine *Trenchant* makes a triumphant return to Fremantle as it passes through the open boom defence net after sinking the Japanese heavy cruiser *Ashigara* in the Malacca Strait on 8 June 1945. The largest warship sunk by a British submarine in World War Two, *Ashigara* had represented Japan at the 1937 Coronation Review at Spithead. The wartime censor has deleted the gun emplacements, searchlights, boom defence facilities and buildings on the South Mole in this photograph. *(Author's collection)*

The two destroyers *Armada* and the Tribal class **HMAS Warramunga** (rear) moored in Farm Cove, Sydney harbour on 11 January 1946. One of the early Battle class destroyers, *Armada* was constructed by Hawthorn Leslie and completed in July 1945, just months before this photograph was taken. She was sold on 12 November 1965 and broken up at Inverkeithing.

(*John Mortimer*)

A detailed view of the submarine depot ship **Adamant** in Sydney on 25 June 1946, with her "flock" of seven boats. The ship was berthed in Athol Bight, across the harbour from the Garden Island Naval Dockyard. Two of **Adamant's** twin 4.5-inch guns, at maximum elevation, are visible on the left. The ship was a member of the British Pacific Fleet. Listed for disposal in 1966, **Adamant** was scrapped from September 1970.

(*John Mortimer*)

Another visitor to Sydney, Australia's main east coast port was **Veryan Bay**. The frigate was armed with two twin 4-inch guns and two twin 40mm Bofors and, for anti-submarine attacks, one hedgehog, depth charge rails and throwers (right aft). **Veryan Bay** was broken up in 1959.

(*John Mortimer*)

The Ruler class escort/ferry aircraft carrier **Atheling** alongside the RAN reserve dolphins at Athol Bight in Sydney on 31 December 1945. Commissioned as **USS Glacier** in Puget Sound on 3 July 1943, she was handed over to the Royal Navy 28 days later - on 31 July and commissioned as *Atheling* after modifications in Vancouver. She served in home waters before proceeding to the Indian Ocean. She was returned to the USN in 1946. **Atheling** was sold as the mercantile **Roma** in 1950 and broken-up in 1967. (*Fleet Air Arm Museum Archive*)

A very popular aircraft carrier, *Formidable* berthing at Circular Quay, Sydney Harbour. A huge crowd of well-wishers greet the crew, many of whom are on the forward flight deck. Laid down on 17 June 1937, launched on 17 August 1939 and completed on 24 November 1940, she was one of three Illustrious class fleet carriers to enter service from May 1940 to May 1941. She ended her career in 1953, broken up, after a decision that no further upgrades would be carried out on the carrier. (*Fleet Air Arm Museum Archive*)

The fleet carrier **Implacable** proceeding to its berth at Wooloomooloo in Sydney in November, 1945. She was employed ferrying Australian troops from Wewak, New Guinea back home. **Implacable** later repatriated Allied former POWs to Australia and Canada from Japan. She sailed for the UK from Sydney after a local refit on 5 May, 1946.

(*Fleet Air Arm Museum Archive*)

The light fleet aircraft carrier **Venerable** alongside the Athol Bight "dolphins" in 1945. Sydney provided a major maintenance facility for many units of the British Pacific Fleet. One of ten Colossus class carriers to be completed by April 1946, **Venerable** served with the "senior service" until 1948, and was then transferred to the Netherlands as the **Karel Doorman**.

(*Fleet Air Arm Museum Archive*)

The aircraft component repair ship *Deer Sound* seen in Mosman Bay, Sydney holding Divisions on a Sunday morning in December 1945. She had recently arrived from Hong Kong. The bulges on the stern are a legacy of the ship's previous role (when named *Port Quebec)* as a minelayer. These bulges were later turned into the ship's laundry. *Deer Sound* had been part of the Pacific Fleet Train.

(Fleet Air Arm Museum Archive)

The aircraft carrier *Victorious* departs from alongside a Woolloomooloo wharf, just south of Garden Island. Four of the carrier's twin 4.5-inch guns are raised to maximum elevation. The ship was returning to England with additional personnel, including WRNS, seen on the forward end of the flight deck. The rebuilt *Victorious* would later return for further service in the Far East during the 1950s and 1960s, and visit several Australian ports.

(Fleet Air Arm Museum Archive)

A very busy Woolloomooloo Bay, Sydney Harbour in late 1945. Two unidentified Fleet destroyers from the British Pacific Fleet lie alongside the wharves, with two Illustrious / Implacable class Fleet Carriers in the background. During the later stages of the conflict, Sydney Harbour provided the main port facilities for the impressive number of ships that formed the British Pacific Fleet. Fighting ships and support vessels were berthed or anchored around and in the numerous bays, all protected from enemy attack by the boom defence net placed just a short distance from the famous Sydney 'Heads'.

(Author's Collection)

A view taken aboard *Illustrious*, with her crew in winter rig, at the war's end in late 1945. The White Ensign proudly flies from the ship's stern. *Illustrious* was completed in May 1940 and experienced a very hard war, surviving an attack by seven bomb hits and a near miss on 10 January 1941, when almost 8,000lbs of bombs hit the armoured deck. The ship was scrapped in 1956.

(*Fleet Air Arm Museum Archive*)

During the Second World War, the Royal Navy manned four of the new landing ships dock (LSDs) originally designed for service in the United States Navy. Provided under the "Lend-Lease" scheme from the USA, *Oceanway* (ex *Dagger*, ex *LSD 12*, ex *BAP M4)* was returned post war. She is shown here about to sail below the Sydney Harbour Bridge for a maintenance visit.

(Fleet Air Arm Museum Archive)

The light fleet carrier **Theseus** visiting the Port of Melbourne in 1947. The carrier was opened to the public, with thousands of visitors taking the opportunity to visit the light fleet carrier. The need to take large numbers of Royal Marines and their equipment to sea was carried out by the Royal Navy using **Theseus** nine years later during the Suez Crisis. The commando assault, the first ever "vertical envelopment", included 415 marines and 23 tons of stores placed ashore by Whirlwind helicopters from the modified carriers **Theseus** and **Ocean** at Port Said, Egypt on 3 November 1956, having been hastily modified for the assault role. **Theseus** then returned to England in December to be placed into extended reserve. She was sold in 1961.

(Fleet Air Arm Museum Archive)

The T-class submarine *Taurus* refitting on the Western Australian Government Public Works Slipway No.1 in Fremantle on 14 July 1946. Based at Ceylon and later Fremantle, *Taurus* sank the Japanese submarine *I-34* in the Malacca Straits on 12 November 1943. Loaned to the Royal Netherlands Navy in 1948 and re-named *Dolfjin*, she was returned to the Royal Navy in 1953 and finally broken-up in 1960.

(*Walter Murray*)

The somewhat weather-beaten Flagship of the 4th Cruiser Squadron, *Swiftsure*, alongside Victoria Quay in the Port of Fremantle on 14 July, 1946. The Japanese surrender of Hong Kong had been signed onboard on 16 September, 1945.
(*Walter Murray*)

The light fleet carrier *Theseus* in Sydney in 1947. A few of the Colossus class carriers were built just in time to deploy to the Pacific Ocean in the later stages of the Second World War, but none experienced any significant combat operations. Postwar they provided the nucleus of three Commonwealth and a number of other friendly navies, serving as front-line ships, trials or training carriers. *Colossus*, was transferred to France in August 1946 and then sold outright in 1951, *Venerable* was sold to the Netherlands in May 1948, *Vengeance* to Brazil in December 1956 and finally, *Warrior* to Argentina in July 1958.

(Fleet Air Arm Museum Archive)

The Town class cruiser *Newcastle* about to sail beneath the Sydney Harbour Bridge. The cruiser then berthed at Garden Island. Like many other ships before, many captains wanted their warship photographed beneath the bridge, as a publicity shot. *Newcastle*, a Southampton class cruiser served for a total of 21 years, between completion on 5 March 1937 and paying off in 1958. She was broken up at Faslane in 1959.

(*John Mortimer*)

The submarine *Talent* about to berth at Garden Island. The boat's single four inch gun is visible in front of the conning tower. Two of the bow 21 inch torpedo tubes can also be seen. The T class submarine was built by Vickers-Armstrong at Barrow and launched on 13 February 1945. *Talent* was armed with a total of eleven 21 inch tubes, including six internal bow and five external tubes. A total of 17 torpedoes were normally carried, including the five "fish" in the external tubes. In 1956 *Talent's* conning tower was severely damaged when she was hit by a merchant ship, whilst dived off St. Catherine's Head (Isle of Wight). *Talent* survived until 1969, before being broken up.

(John Mortimer)

Wearing her peacetime livery, and before the fitting of its minelaying rails, the C-class destroyer **Comet** is seen underway in Fremantle Harbour in August, 1946.   (*Walter Murray*)

With five LCMs embarked along with various other equipment and Army personnel, the LST *Narvik* departs from Fremantle on 22 April 1952 in support of "Operation Hurricane", the British atomic tests at the Monte Bello Islands off the West Australian coast.

(Courtesy of WA Newspapers)

Fully laden with landing craft and equipment, the LST *Zeebrugge* departing Fremantle on 22 April 1952 after a six-day stopover. *Zeebrugge* was bound for the Monte Bello Islands off the northern coast of Western Australia and the site of "Operation Hurricane" - the British atomic tests.

(Courtesy of WA Newspapers)

The flagship of the Far Eastern Fleet, the aircraft carrier **Ark Royal** is seen departing the Port of Fremantle in 1962 after a highly popular goodwill visit. (*Fremantle Port Authority*)

"Dress Ship" was the Order-of-the-day with the Royal Yacht **Gothic** alongside in the Port of Fremantle during HRH Queen Elizabeth's 1954 visit to Australia. Forward of **Gothic** are the two RAN minesweepers, **HMA Ships Fremantle** (outboard) and **Junee**. Astern is the escorting destroyer **HMAS Bataan**. *(Author's collection)*

HRH Queen Elizabeth II and the Duke of Edinburgh, embarked on the (temporary) Royal Yacht **Gothic**, are given the traditional "Three Cheers" by the ship's company of the escorting aircraft carrier **HMAS Vengeance** off Cocos Island in the Indian Ocean on 5 April 1954. **Vengeance** was on loan to the RAN between 1952-55 until **HMAS Melbourne** was completed.

(*RAN*)

The Singapore-based Far Eastern Fleet Flagship of the 5th Cruiser Squadron *Newfoundland* proceeding to sea after a visit to the Port of Fremantle in Western Australia on 1 June 1956. Five months later on 1 November *Newfoundland,* in company with *Diana,* sank the Egyptian frigate *Domiat*, by gunfire, in the Gulf of Suez during the 1956 Suez crisis.

(*Author's collection*)

The Royal Fleet Auxiliary tanker *Wave Ruler* anchored in the Port of Fremantle inner harbour in 1959 in company with the aircraft carrier *Albion*. The *Wave Ruler* was originally launched as the *Empire Eversham* on 17 January, 1946 and was finally reduced to a hulk in 1970.

(Author's Collection)

In 1959 the City of Brisbane in the State of Queensland held its Centenary celebrations. The aircraft carrier *Centaur* was to play an important part in the celebrations. She is shown here steaming up the Brisbane River, some of her crew on the forward flight deck spelling out, "BRISBANE 1859-1959". *(Fleet Air Arm Museum Archive)*

The year is 1961 and the Loch class frigate *Loch Killisport* arrives in Sydney Cove. One of 30 Loch class laid down during the Second World War, *Loch Killisport* was constructed by Harland and Wolff in Belfast and launched on 6 July 1944. Her top speed was 19.5 knots and her normal crew consisted of 114 officers and men. She was one of the last of her class in commission with the Royal Navy and was not broken up until 1970.

(John Mortimer)

In the postwar years before the British withdrawal from Singapore, billowing Union Jack's aboard Royal Navy warships were a very common sight in the Port of Fremantle in Western Australia. This 1959 photograph shows the destroyer **Cavalier** as a unit of the 8th Destroyer Squadron outboard of an unidentified frigate at North Wharf. *(Author's Collection)*

The Commonwealth connection. Seen at North Wharf, Fremantle in 1959 are three British design and two British-built Commonwealth warships. The Type 61 frigate **HMS Chichester** is outboard of the Australian Daring-class destroyer **HMAS Voyager** (Australian-built) and the Bellona-class light cruiser **HMNZS** (former **HMS**, transferred 1954) **Royalist**.

(Author's Collection)

The Far Eastern Fleet light fleet carrier **Albion** alongside at North Wharf, Fremantle in 1959. Visible on the flight deck are Sea Venom aircraft. Astern of **Albion** is the RAN aircraft carrier **HMAS Melbourne**.

(Author's Collection)

A unit of the Sydney-based Royal Navy 4th Submarine Squadron, the "super streamlined" *Trump* participating in winching exercises with an RAN Fleet Air Arm Iroquois of 723 Squadron off Jervis Bay, New South Wales in the mid-1960s. *Trump* was the last RN submarine to be based in Australia, leaving in January 1969 after Australia re-formed its own submarine service.

(*RAN*)

A 1960s view of the Singapore-based Far Eastern Fleet aircraft carrier *Eagle* with the submarine *Oberon* in the foreground, at the RAN Garden Island Naval Dockyard, Sydney.   (*RAN*)

The Singapore-based World War Two and Korean War veteran *Belfast* underway in Sydney Harbour on 14 September 1961 during her 1959-62 Far East deployment. (*RAN*)

A popular visitor, the Singapore-based Far Eastern Fleet cruiser *Tiger* alongside at North Wharf in Fremantle during the 1962 Commonwealth Games. *(Author's Collection)*

The modernised Illustrious class fleet carrier *Victorious* was a regular member of the Far East Fleet, based in Singapore up to 1966. After a number of wartime visits to Australian cities, *Victorious* returned to Sydney in 1966, as "flagship" of a five ship task group. The visit would turn out to be her last. After her return to the United Kingdom, *Victorious* suffered a minor fire whilst in refit on 11 November 1967. Due to politically inspired force level cuts to the Royal Navy, it was decided not to repair the damage and the ship decommissioned on 13 March 1968. *Victorious* was sold in July 1969 and scrapped at Faslane. (*Fleet Air Arm Museum Archive*)

The "Ca" class destroyer, **Caprice**, was originally completed in April 1944, but upgraded in the mid 1950s, during regular maintenance periods. By 1966 the ship's armament was three 4.5-inch guns and two single 40mm guns. With her torpedo tubes removed amidships, the topside weight saved was taken up by a quadruple launcher for Seacat anti-aircraft missiles. Two Squid triple anti-submarine mortars were also fitted. **Caprice's** final commission ended in March 1973. She was broken up in Queenborough from November 1979. (*RAN*)

Another "grand" tour of Sydney Harbour. This time the Type 15 anti-submarine frigate *Zest* sails up Port Jackson, with the Opera House (still under construction) in the background. Originally one of eight Z class destroyers, *Zest* emerged from her 1954-55 rebuild at Chatham Dockyard, armed with one twin 4-inch gun (aft), one twin 40mm Bofors (forward of bridge) and two triple barrelled Limbo anti-submarine mortars on the quarterdeck. The original planned torpedo tubes were never fitted. *Zest* and other similar conversions provided a strong deterrent to the Soviet submarine threat of the late 1950s and 1960s, until they were eventually replaced by the purpose designed Whitby, Rothesay and Leander class frigates. *Zest* was sold for scrapping in 1970.

(Steve Bush Collection)

HM Submarine Tabard was one of seven T class boats to serve in Australian waters as part of the Royal Navy's Fourth Submarine Flotilla. The upgraded ***Tabard*** had received a major half-life refit in the early 1950s, prior to arrival in Sydney, her homeport for seven years and four months. ***Tabard*** and her sisters were eventually replaced by the RAN's own Oberon class submarines, the first of which, ***HMAS Oxley*** arrived from her Scottish builders in 1967. After her return from Australia ***Tabard*** enjoyed an extended lease of life as a harbour training vessel at Fort Blockhouse, Gosport, before joining the other T boats at the breakers in March 1974. *(RAN)*

A unit of the Far Eastern Fleet, the commando carrier **Bulwark**, streaming her Paying-Off pennant departs Fremantle in mid-1965, bound for Plymouth and a refit. **Bulwark** was recommissioned again at Plymouth on 22 April 1966.

(Fremantle Port Authority)

A unit of the Far Eastern Fleet, the Tribal-class frigate **Eskimo** departs the Port of Fremantle in the mid-1960s. This class was designed for service in the tropical waters of the West Indies and the Persian Gulf, incorporatng air conditioning from the outset. **Eskimo** is seen wearing the funnel badge of the 9th Frigate Squadron, which operated in the Persian Gulf. It was a widely held belief that these ships were designed with two funnels as, in Arab eyes, a ships prestige was measured by the number of funnels! **Eskimo** was broken-up in 1992.

(Martin Navarro)

A unit of the Far Eastern Fleet, the commando carrier **Bulwark** departing Brisbane, Queensland on 15 November, 1966. **Bulwark** had embarked 845 Naval Air Squadron (Wessex 5 helicopters) from Borneo at the end of Confrontation before proceeding to Australian waters to participate in "Exercise Barrawinga" off Queensland.   (*Fleet Air Arm Museum Archive*)

In the twilight of her career and as a unit of the Far Eastern Fleet, the large destroyer ***Daring*** arrives in Sydney during her 1967-68 commission before being placed in reserve in 1968. ***Daring*** was broken-up at Blyth in 1971.

(Author's Collection)

The Far Eastern Fleet commando carrier **Albion** entering the Port of Fremantle on 18 July 1968 with tug **Walana** leading the way.

(*Martin Navarro*)

HMS Cavendish in Woolloomooloo Bay, Sydney Harbour during the mid 1960s. Laid down on 28 February 1943 and launched on 12 April 1944, the ship was completed for service in December 1944. **Cavendish** began a major modernisation in January 1954, having been brought forward from the Reserve Fleet. The upgrade was designed to provide a ship capable of defending a carrier task force, from Soviet air and submarine attacks. **Cavendish** was broken up in 1967.

(Author's Collection)

The Far Eastern Fleet light fleet carrier **Hermes** berthing at Victoria Quay, Fremantle on 18 February, 1969. She was returning to Portsmouth via Fremantle and Capetown on what was to be her last visit to Western Australia.

(*Fremantle Port Authority*)

The four anti-aircraft frigates of the Leopard class were the most heavily gun-armed frigates in the Royal Navy. At the time their 2,520 tons full load displacement, *Jaguar* (above) and her sisters mounted two twin 4.5-inch guns, one single 40mm Bofors gun and one Squid anti-submarine mortar. After the arrival of additional Leander class general purpose frigates, the specialist frigates such as *Jaguar* were progressively retired from frontline activities. On 6 July 1978 the 19 year old frigate was transferred to Bangladesh and renamed *Ali Haider*. In 2001 she was reported to have been withdrawn from active service.

(*John Mortimer*)

The veteran Royal Navy frigate **Whitby** entering Sydney Harbour on 11 May 1970. Her two 3-barrelled Limbo anti-submarine mortars are just visible in the sheltered well in the after quarter of the ship. Paid-off in 1975, **Whitby** was broken-up in 1979.

(*RAN*)

Accompanying the visit of *Victorious* to Sydney in 1966 was the Royal Fleet Auxiliary *Reliant*. Completed as a merchant ship in 1955, the 7,298 ton *Reliant* was purchased and converted to an aviation support ship to accompany the "Strike" carrier task groups for service mainly in the Far East. She was affectionately known by those serving onboard as "The Yacht". Living conditions onboard were particularly good. She was laid up in 1972 and four years later was sold for scrap.

(*RAN*)

In late 1968, *Fife* visited Sydney. On the right, alongside Garden Island is the River class frigate **HMAS Derwent** (F22) and the Leander class frigate **Argonaut**. The County class guided missile destroyer entered service on 21 June 1966. Under refit at the time of Falklands war, *Fife* emerged in 1983 with the provision to operate a Lynx helicopter, in lieu of the old Wessex. In 1986 her massive Seaslug missile launcher was removed and the magazine converted to a mess deck for cadets under training. In June 1987 *Fife* was decommissioned by the Royal Navy and sold, in August, to Chile. She was refitted in late 1988 with an enlarged helicopter deck and hangar for two aircraft. She is still (2002) active as the **Blanco Encalada**.   (*RAN*)

The **Hermes** Task Group at Garden Island in 1968. The carrier lies alongside the oil wharf at the top of the photograph. Alongside the cruiser wharf is the County class destroyer **Glamorgan**, the Daring class **Diana** (outboard), an RAN Leander class frigate and the Battle class destroyer (training ship) **HMAS Anzac** (outboard). The RAN's last operational Type 15 frigate (training ship) **HMAS Queenborough** is about to berth alongside.

(RAN)

This photograph of *Kent* was taken by the ship's Wessex helicopter, during her departure from Sydney. *Kent* was the second County class guided missile destroyer built for the Royal Navy, completed on 15 August 1963. In 1976 she was severely damaged by fire during a refit at Portsmouth. Although repaired at Wallsend, *Kent* assumed the role of harbour training ship, then as an accommodation ship in Portsmouth and finally as Sea Cadet Corps training ship.

(*Fleet Air Arm Museum Archive*)

The helicopter cruiser **Blake** arriving in Sydney on 11 May 1970 during a Far East deployment. Completed as a cruiser in 1961 and converted to this configuration at Portsmouth between 1965-69, **Blake** was paid-off in December, 1979 and was finally broken-up at Cairnryan in 1982. **Blake** was the last operational cruiser in the Royal Navy.   (*RAN*)

On 14 October 1968, the Daring class destroyer **Diana** is seen arriving in Sydney. After her service in the Royal Navy, **Diana** was sold to Peru in November 1969. Renamed **Palacios** she remained active until stricken in 1993, an incredible 39 years! During her time under the Peruvian flag, the ship was modified with a new plated foremast and space between the after funnel and "X" turret was used for eight fixed Exocet surface to surface missiles. Later, during 1977-78, she had her after 4.5 inch mounting, Squid mortar and two of the Exocets removed to make room for a helicopter landing deck. Her single 40mm guns were also replaced by Breda twin 40mm mountings.

(John Mortimer)

The Singapore-based general purpose frigate **Mermaid** with its somewhat rare Mk XIX twin 4-inch gun mount forward, departing Fremantle in the mid-1970s after a goodwill visit. Laid down for the Ghanaian Navy and cancelled when almost complete, it was eventually completed by Yarrow Shipbuilders and laid-up in 1968 until its eventual acceptance by the Royal Navy in 1972. **Mermaid** was sold to the Malaysian Navy only five years later and renamed **Hang Tuah**. (*Fremantle Port Authority*)

A unit of the highly successful Porpoise-class submarines, *Finwhale* is seen departing Fremantle after a goodwill visit in the 1970s. *(Martin Navarro)*

The 20 year old aircraft carrier *Eagle* about to sail through Sydney "Heads" on 9 August 1971 on her final visit to Australia. Having completed a major rebuild in 1964 *Eagle* remained a most modern carrier when the decision was announced to withdraw her from service, on the pretext it would cost too much to convert her to operate the more sophisticated Phantom aircraft. Accordingly, *Eagle* was paid off in January 1972. Laid up in Devonport for the next six years, she was eventually towed to the breakers in 1978. (*John Mortimer*)

In the twilight days of the Royal Navy presence in the Far East, the commando carrier *Albion* is seen berthed alongside Victoria Quay in Fremantle on 10 August 1971. She was to be part of the British Far Eastern Fleet withdrawal from Singapore just two months later.

(Fremantle Port Authority)

The guided-missile destroyer **Devonshire**, still maintaining its original appearance, departing Fremantle on 4 December 1972 after a goodwill visit. After a relatively short operational life of 18 years she was expended as a target in 1984. She was sunk in the North Atlantic by a Tigerfish torpedo fired from the nuclear powered submarine *Splendid*.

(*Martin Navarro*)

The last Royal Navy submarine to enter the Port of Fremantle's inner harbour, **Odin**, is seen departing the port on 5 December 1973. **Odin's** sister **Opossum** was the last conventionally powered RN submarine to visit Western Australia, visiting the nearby **HMAS Stirling** naval base in November, 1990. Since then, all (nuclear-powered) Royal Navy submarine visits have been to the **HMAS Stirling** Fleet Base at Garden Island in Cockburn Sound - south of Fremantle.

(Fremantle Port Authority)

HM Ships Fife and ***Argonaut*** depart Sydney on 3 June 1974. The Leander class frigate ***Argonaut*** was almost the last of the original 16 ship Leander class frigates to be completed - in August 1967. In March 1980 ***Argonaut*** emerged from refit as a "new" ship, converted to fire Exocet anti-ship missiles with the original twin 4.5-inch gun mounting removed. Facilities to operate the new Lynx helicopter, plus three Seacat missile launchers and two single 40mm Bofor guns were added. ***Argonaut*** was damaged by bombs during the Falklands conflict. She was listed for disposal in 1993.

(*John Mortimer*)

The County class guided missile destroyer **Glamorgan** leads a group of Royal Navy ships up Sydney Harbour beneath the Sydney Harbour Bridge. The ships then sailed around the Cockatoo Island Dockyard to return down harbour to their berths at Garden Island, just visible to the right. **Glamorgan** was in the active RN fleet between October 1966 and September 1986. She was then sold to Chile in October 1986, where she remained active as the **Almirante Latorre** until 30 December 1998.

(*RAN*)

RFA Tidespring sails into Sydney Harbour on 28 November 1975. Built as a member of the Tide class (second group), the ship was completed in 1963. Three years later she supported the Biera Patrol and in 1976, participated in the "Cod War". **Tidespring** was sold to Chile in 1982 and renamed **Almirante Jorge Montt**. (*John Mortimer*)

The Royal Yacht **Britannia** was a regular visitor to Sydney's harbour over four decades. In this view she is seen being escorted up to her normal berth in Sydney Cove, opposite the Opera House. As one of the few to embark in the ship whilst in Australia, the authors can vouch for the ship's immaculate appearance. **Britannia** was in commission from January 1954. After a world-wide career the yacht was moved to Edinburgh in 1998 and opened for public inspection.

(*Author's Collection*)

The converted helicopter cruiser *Tiger* made a splendid sight as she proceeded down Sydney Harbour on 19 December 1977. Originally laid down in October 1941, but not commissioned until 1959, the ship was refitted (1968-72) to enable her to embark up to four Sea King helicopters. She was also fitted with two quadruple launchers for Seacat missiles. She retained one of her two twin six-inch and one of the three twin three-inch guns. *Tiger* paid off in April 1978 and was sold in 1986 to be broken up in Spain. (*John Mortimer*)

The Royal Fleet Auxiliary replenishment ship **Regent** entering the Port of Fremantle on 5 November 1983 as part of the "Orient Express" Far East Task Group. (*RAN*)

The Leander-class frigate *Aurora* glides into Fremantle Harbour between a sheep carrier in the foreground and the Knutsen Line's **Elisabeth Bakke** visible at North Wharf on 5 November, 1983. A unit of the visiting "Orient Express" task group, *Aurora* was proceeding to her berth at Victoria Quay.
(*RAN*)

The veteran anti-submarine frigate **HMS Rothesay** entering Fremantle Harbour as part of the "Orient Express" Far East Group deployment on 5 November 1983. *Rothesay* was broken-up in 1987.

(*RAN*)

The immaculate Royal Yacht **Britannia** berthing at Victoria Quay, Fremantle on 21 March 1986. No members of the Royal Family were embarked at the time. (*RAN*)

One of the Royal Navy's new Invincible class light carriers visited Sydney for the first time in December 1984. *Invincible* proved extremely popular when open to the public. The ship's twin Sea Dart missile launcher can be seen on the starboard bow and aft, the Phalanx close-in-weapon-system.

(Fleet Air Arm Museum Archive)

Escorted by a police launch, the aircraft carrier *Illustrious* glides past the North Mole as it enters Fremantle's inner harbour for its first visit on 25 October 1986. *Illustrious* was the Flagship of the "Global 86" Group Deployment.

(*RAN*)

For the RAN's 75th Anniversary celebrations, the Royal Navy provided a small fleet, including the Type 22 frigate **Beaver**, (shown here), as well as ***Illustrious***, ***Manchester***, ***Amazon*** and ***RFA Fort Grange***. Equipped with only two single 40mm guns, the frigate **Beaver** was missile armed, including two sextuple Seawolf missile launchers for anti-air and anti-missile defence and four Exocet surface to surface missiles. She was paid off early and scrapped in 2001

(RAN)

HMS Invincible anchored in Sydney Harbour on 4 October 1986. The aircraft carrier and her escorting Task Group visited Sydney as part of the 75th Anniversary celebrations of the establishment of the Royal Australian Navy in 1911. The fleet of warships was reviewed by HRH Prince Philip, the Duke of Edinburgh. During the visit, ***Invincible's*** air group was detached to the Naval Air Station, ***HMAS Albatross***.

(*RAN*)

The Type 21 frigate, *Amazon*, off Sydney on 28 September 1986. The crew were preparing to man ship for the ceremonial entry into harbour.

(*John Mortimer*)

The Type 42 Batch III guided-missile destroyer *Manchester* entering Fremantle Harbour on 25 October 1986. She was another unit of the "Global 86" Task Group which participated in the RAN's 75th Anniversary Fleet Review in Sydney.
(*RAN*)

A long way from home.......The two small Hong Kong patrol vessels **Starling** and **Plover** (inboard) are seen alongside Victoria Quay in Fremantle after their arrival on a goodwill visit on 3 February 1987.

(*RAN*)

The aircraft carrier *Ark Royal* entering the Port of Fremantle on 23 October 1988.

(*RAN*)

RFA Olwen passes the Sydney Opera House in October 1988. ***Olwen*** and a number of other warships and auxiliaries were "in town" as part of the Bicentennial Naval Review. His Royal Highness, Prince Andrew was the Reviewing Officer. ***Olwen*** began her long career in 1965, the first of three Olwen class, an improved version of the earlier Tide class fleet tankers.

(*John Mortimer*)

The guided-missile destroyer ***Edinburgh*** arrives in Sydney as part of the ***Ark Royal*** task group visiting Australia for its Bicentennial Fleet Review in Sydney.

(*RAN*)

*HMS **Illustrious*** at anchor off Neutral Bay in Sydney Harbour. Taken in October 1988, the carrier was moved into the harbour for the formal Royal Review. ***Illustrious*** shared the main review line with the French cruiser ***Colbert*** and the American battleship ***USS New Jersey***. *(RAN)*

RFA Fort Grange moves past North Mole as it prepares to enter Fremantle Harbour on 23 October 1988. She was also part of the **Ark Royal** task group visiting Australia for the Bicentennial celebrations.
(*RAN*)

The modified Leander class frigate *Sirius* proceeds slowly up Sydney Harbour in October 1988. Completed on 15 June 1966 the frigate underwent a major half-life modernisation during 1975-77, including the fitting of Exocet missiles. Towed array sonar was fitted in 1981-83. Paid off on 27 February 1993, *Sirius* was towed to Milford Haven in July 1996 and later sunk as a target.

(John Mortimer)

HM Submarine *Opossum* berthing at Oxley Wharf at the RAN's Fleet Base West, ***HMAS Stirling*** at Garden Island, Western Australia on 29 November 1990. ***Opossum*** was the first Royal Navy submarine to visit the base - the home of the Australian Submarine Squadron - since it was commissioned in 1978. (*RAN*)

One of the few Royal Navy visitors seen "down under" in the recent past was the guided-missile frigate ***Boxer***. She is seen here entering Fremantle Harbour on 8 October, 1992.

(*Author's Collection*)

The third Invincible class carrier to visit Sydney was ***Ark Royal***, seen here berthing alongside the Sydney Cove Passenger terminal in 1990. *(Fleet Air Arm Museum Archive)*

The first Royal Navy nuclear-powered submarine to visit Australia was the Trafalgar-class *Triumph* seen here arriving at the **HMAS Stirling** naval base in Western Australia on 11 May 1993.

(*RAN*)

The nuclear-powered submarine *Trenchant* proceeding to sea from *HMAS Stirling* - Fleet Base West at Garden Island, Western Australia on 17 July 1997. *Trenchant's* sister, *Trafalgar* (foreground) salutes the departing submarine.

(*RAN*)

The Type 23 guided-missile frigate **Richmond** arriving in Fremantle on 14 July 1997 whilst on a Far East deployment. *(RAN)*

Index